Edexcel GCSE (9-1) Business

Theme 2: Building a business

About you

Name: _____

Class: _____

Teacher(s): _____

Lessons: _____

Contents

Theme 2 Building a business

Topic 2.1 Growing the business
2.1.1 Business growth 5
2.1.2 Changes in business aims and objectives 12
2.1.3 Business and globalisation 17
2.1.4 Ethics, the environment and business 24

Topic 2.2 Making marketing decisions
2.2.1 Product 31
2.2.2 Price 36
2.2.3 Promotion 41
2.2.4 Place 45
2.2.5 Using the marketing mix to make business decisions ... 48

Topic 2.3 Making operational decisions
2.3.1 Business operations 52
2.3.2 Working with suppliers 58
2.3.3 Managing quality 64
2.3.4 The sales process 69

Topic 2.4 Making financial decisions
2.4.1 Business calculations 73
2.4.2 Understanding business performance 78

Topic 2.5 Making human resource decisions
2.5.1 Organisational structures 84
2.5.2 Effective recruitment 93
2.5.3 Effective training and development 98
2.5.4 Motivation 102

2.1.1 Business growth

What you need to learn
- Methods of business growth and their impact:
  - internal (organic) growth: new products (innovation, research and development), new markets (through changing the marketing mix or taking advantage of technology and/or expanding overseas)
  - external (inorganic) growth: merger, takeover
- The types of business ownership for growing businesses:
  - public limited company (plc)
- Sources of finance for growing and established businesses:
  - internal sources: retained profit, selling assets
  - external sources: loan capital, share capital, including stock market flotation (public limited companies)

Businesses can expand in a number of ways. This can be through **organic growth** or **external growth**.

Organic (internal growth) is growth from within the business. This can be achieved by:
- new products
  - innovation - the development of an idea into a new product or process. Businesses invest time and money in order to make a profit. **Product innovation** occurs through adapting a product that already exists. An innovation is likely to have a patent as the business looks to recoup the cost of research and development by stopping other businesses from copying its product. Often, a small business will sell out to a larger one
  - research and development – scientific research and technical development is expensive, particularly with high fixed costs. This can create barriers to entry and a tendency towards less competition in the market, increasing the market power of the business

- new markets
  - changing the marketing mix – this could be through opening more physical stores (place), making it more convenient for customer; increasing the product range; changing price to help increase market share; increasing promotional spend
  - taking advantage of technology - use of e-commerce and m-commerce to develop sales and markets
  - expanding overseas - selling the same product but abroad. This can be expensive and risky as the business has less understanding of the market. However, there is huge potential reward due to the size of the overseas market

External growth occurs when businesses grow by integrating (joining) with another business. This can be achieved through:
- **A merger** - the businesses reach an agreement to join together and operate as one business
  - Tends to be of mutual benefit to both businesses
- **A takeover** - one business buys another business
  - Tends to be more hostile as the buying business is the main one to benefit

External growth can take different formats depending upon whether the firms involved operate at the same or different stages of production.

Horizontal Integration	Backward Vertical Integration	Forward Vertical Integration
Both firms operate at same stage of the production process e.g. two banks	The firms operate at different stages of the production process.	
	One business joins with another at an earlier stage in the production process e.g. a fashion manufacturer buys a cotton business	One business joins with another at a later stage in the production process e.g. a fashion manufacturer buys a fashion retailer
• Gain market share • Reduces competition • Bigger and more powerful • Stronger negotiating power with suppliers	• Secures the supply of materials • Cuts out a middle layer • Limits supplies to competitors	• Firm is at a later stage in the production process • Secures an outlet for the products • Cuts out a middle layer • Can exclude competitors from that outlet

Another type of external growth is diversification. This occurs when the firms who join together operate in different industries e.g. a car manufacturer integrates with a stationery retailer. This can help spread risk as the business now operates in a range of markets.

Disadvantages of mergers and takeovers:
- Takeovers can be very expensive • Difficult to control due to size
- Different business structures and practices to bring together
- Opposition from stakeholders • Managers may lack experience
- May attract negative publicity, especially if results in job losses

As a business grows it will experience many **benefits** but there are also **risks**.

Benefits of growth	Risks of growth
Increased sales and potential profit	Actions of competitors
Greater market share	More difficult to manage
Greater power to negotiate with suppliers	Coordination and communication issues
Lower unit costs	Need to maintain quality
Better reputation - more known	Growing too quickly may lead to failure
Wider choice of promotional activities	Strain on resources e.g. cash and workforce
Stronger trading position than competitors	

Types of business ownership for growing businesses

As a business grows there is an option to become a **public limited company**.

There are lots of **similarities** between **private** and **public limited companies**:
- Shareholders are the owners of limited companies
- Shareholders have **limited liability**
- Shareholders can only lose the money that they have invested in the business in the form of shares, they are not personally liable for the business' debts
- The business exists in its own right and can therefore be sued as an organisation
- The owners and the company are separate legal entities
- The company's finances are separate from the owner's personal finances
- Registered at Companies House

There are however some important differences between private and public limited companies:
- A public limited company has plc after its name, not ltd

- A plc must have issued at least £50 000 worth of shares
- At least 25% (£12 500) of shares have to be paid for
- A plc can sell shares to the general public
- Shares of a plc are listed on a stock exchange

Sources of finance for growing and established businesses

Internal sources

Retained profits

Profit kept within the business from profit after tax to help finance future activity.
Growing and established businesses are likely to have greater retained profits than start-up businesses.
Increased investment will reduce the amount available for dividends but will yield greater returns if the share price increases.

Advantages	Disadvantages
No interest payments.	May conflict with shareholders who require dividends.
Quick and easy to access.	Dependent on the levels of profit of the business.
Retains control of the business.	May conflict with shareholders who require dividends.
	Dependent on the levels of profit of the business.

Selling assets

An asset is something that is owned by a business e.g. vehicles, land and machinery.
A business can sell off assets that it no longer requires.
Alternatively it may choose to sell off an asset and then lease it back.
This provides an immediate, one-off, cash injection into the business.

Advantages	Disadvantages
No need to repay.	No longer have the option to use the asset.
No interest payments.	Resale value may be low.
No loss of control.	Business must ensure the asset is genuinely unwanted as otherwise a short cash inflow may lead to expensive lease costs in the future.
Disposes of unwanted assets.	

External sources

Loan capital

A set amount of money borrowed from the bank, normally for a specific purpose, to be paid back over a period of time, with a fixed interest rate e.g. 5 years at 6% of the initial sum per annum. Interest has to be paid on the amount borrowed.

A growing business is likely to be less of a risk than a start-up business. This will allow it to obtain cheaper finance from banks.

Advantages	Disadvantages
Lower interest rates than start-up businesses. Quick and easy to access.	A higher proportion of capital invested into the business comes from loans, it is therefore at more risk if interest rates rise.

Flotation

When a company becomes a public limited company it offers its shares to the public for sale, this is called an **Initial Public Offering (IPO).** This process is referred to as **flotation** or **floating** a company.

Advantages	Disadvantages
Flotation on the stock market allows access to a much larger source of finance	Flotation is an expensive process and not guaranteed to be successful
Plcs tend to be large, stable companies meaning it is easier to access further finance from banks	The general public can buy shares meaning that the company is at risk of a hostile takeover
More finance available means greater opportunities for expansion	Financial information is freely available for anyone to see, including competitors
Enhanced reputation of the company due to its plc status	Stricter rules and regulations are placed on plcs
The company gains exposure through a stock exchange	Shareholders are motivated by profit which may cause conflict with other stakeholders e.g. employees and community
	There is potential for conflict due to a **divorce of ownership and control** meaning that the owners of the business, the shareholders, might be different from those who control it, the board of directors

Test Yourself

2.1.1 Business growth

1. Distinguish between organic and inorganic growth.

2. Explain one reason why developing new products can help a business to grow.

3. Explain one reason why developing new markets can help a business to grow.

4. Explain one advantage of growing a business through a merger.

5. Explain one disadvantage of growing a business through a takeover.

6. Explain one reason why becoming a public limited company can help a business to grow.

7. Explain why the following internal sources of finance can help a business to grow:
   a. Retained profit
   b. Selling assets

8. Explain one benefit of using loan capital to expand a business.

9. Explain one benefit of using share capital to expand a business.

10. Explain one reason why business growth through flotation might be a disadvantage to a business.

2.1.2 Changes in business aims and objectives

What you need to learn
- Why business aims and objectives change as businesses evolve:
  - in response to: market conditions, technology, performance, legislation, internal reasons
- How business aims and objectives change as businesses evolve:
  - focus on survival or growth
  - entering or exiting markets
  - growing or reducing the workforce
  - increasing or decreasing product range

Market conditions

Businesses consider the degree of competition in the market. Some competitors will leave the market, perhaps creating opportunities for growth for other established businesses. A lack of competition can help a business to maintain and develop customer loyalty, restrict output and charge higher prices. This might allow it to become a dominant business, benefit from lower costs and become market leader.

The state of the economy will impact on the business. If the economy is in a weak position or a recession this will lead to less demand, impacting on revenues and profit. In a boom a business will look to increase sales and invest in expansion.

Technology

Due to rapid changes in technology new opportunities open for business. The use of e-commerce to drive sales can lead to growth. Businesses can access larger markets and distribute products more easily. Processes, used to produce products, have improved. This makes it quicker and easier for the business to produce, whilst lowering unit costs.

However, technology has also created threats with increased competition and heavy investment from large competitors, such as Amazon and Uber, destroying other businesses in the market. These businesses constantly invest in research and development, creating new products to increase market share.

Performance

Poor business performance e.g. in terms of sales might make a business consider its position in the market. Some businesses will decide to leave the market. Those that stay will have to invest in resources in order to increase sales.

Other businesses might be successful in the market and look to grow further. This will require investment in resources, such as staffing and marketing. Increases in size should reduce unit costs, leading to higher profit margins per unit sold.

Legislation

Changes in the law mean that some businesses have no option but to change their aims and objectives. The Government regularly introduce new legislation that businesses must comply with. The degree to which these laws impact depend on the nature of the business. For example, the tobacco industry has been hit hard by legislation stopping people smoking in public places. This has led to a decline in sales. Tobacco companies have targeted new markets, such as Africa, where laws are not as strict. Businesses will also take account of changes to legislation in consumer law and employment law e.g. the national minimum wage.

Internal influences

Businesses might change their aims and objectives due to reasons within the organisation. New leadership could lead to a change in the direction of the business. The new leader will have their own ideas and might quickly look to make changes in order to improve performance e.g. reducing the size of the business in order to cut costs and increase profits.

The culture of the organisation might see gradual or rapid change in response to changes in the external environment, such as the economy. This will depend on a number of influences within the business, including:

- Leadership, such as the founder of the business leaving
- Personalities, particularly senior directors
- The mission statement, which sets out the overall goal of the business
- The influence of various stakeholders, such as shareholders and customers

How business aims and objectives change as businesses evolve:

Focus on survival or growth

Many businesses make losses at some time, dependent on a range of factors such as the state of the economy and level of competition in the market.

Once established, most businesses will look to grow:
- This will lead to greater rewards for the owners of the business as they seek new markets and develop new products
- It will also lead to financial and non-financial motivators for senior managers. These will see increased pay and bonuses
- They will also have greater recognition and self-esteem, as they are in charge of larger departments in bigger businesses

Not all businesses will look to grow. Some, particularly family run businesses, will be satisfied with a certain level of profit. This allows them to pursue other objectives such as leisure activities.

Many businesses make losses at some time, dependent on a range of factors such as the state of the economy and level of competition in the market. Clearly, survival is the first aim of all businesses as they would not exist otherwise.

Entering or exiting markets

Businesses constantly monitor and review the markets in which they operate.

New opportunities may arise:
- Geographical markets, such as China and India, offer greater scope for growth
- Therefore, businesses might invest in resources to access these markets in return for significant rewards
- Businesses will also look to develop new products. This will depend on changing trends in their current market

Threats mean that some businesses will exit markets:
- The entry of large new competitors into a market will impact significantly on established businesses
- They might struggle to maintain market share as competitors eat into market share

- This was seen in the book market when Amazon undercut traditional bookshops with its low cost strategy, meaning that it could charge lower prices than stores that had a physical presence on the high street

Growing or reducing the workforce

Businesses might look to increase the size of its workforce:
- This will be in response to new opportunities that allow the business to increase sales
- By taking on new employees the business is seeking to meet increased demand for its goods and services
- This will require significant financial resources

Alternatively, the business might look to lay off workers:
- If demand for its product has fallen the business might have no alternative but to reduce the size of the workforce
- The business will face resistance as this is detrimental to employees
- However, cutting costs might be necessary for the survival of the business

Increasing or decreasing product range

Businesses might look to increase the product range that they sell
- This will often be based on established products
- The business can then build upon its brand awareness
- This will make it easier to increase sales as there will already be an element of brand loyalty and repeat custom

Alternatively, some businesses might decrease the range of products that they sell
- This might be in response to lower sales
- However, the business might wish to concentrate on its core products
- This would provide greater focus for employees and other stakeholders
- It could sell other products off to increase revenues

Test Yourself

2.1.2 Changes in business aims and objectives

1. Explain one reason market conditions might cause a business to change its aims and objectives.

2. Explain one reason why changes in technology might cause a business to change its aims and objectives.

3. Explain one reason why poor performance might cause a business to change its aims and objectives.

4. Explain one reason why changes in legislation might cause a business to change its aims and objectives.

5. Explain how new leadership might cause a business to change its aims and objectives.

6. Explain why internal changes might cause a business to change its aims and objectives.

7. Explain why a business' aims and objectives might evolve due to a focus on growth.

8. Explain why a business' aims and objectives might evolve due to entering new markets.

9. Explain why a business' aims and objectives might evolve due to a growing workforce.

10. Explain why a business' aims and objectives might evolve due to an increasing product range.

2.1.3 Business and globalisation

What you need to learn
- The impact of globalisation on businesses:
  - imports: competition from overseas, buying from overseas
  - exports: selling to overseas markets
  - changing business locations
  - multinationals
- Barriers to international trade:
  - tariffs
  - trade blocs
- How businesses compete internationally:
  - the use of the internet and e-commerce
  - changing the marketing mix to compete internationally

Globalisation is the increasing interdependence between countries around the world as a result of international trade and working practices.

It has resulted in a greater dependence on global trade, an increase in the number of transnational companies and more movement of employees, goods and services between countries.

Globalisation has meant increased competition for UK businesses but also an opportunity to compete internationally. UK businesses compete internationally by:

- Better designs
- Higher quality products at lower prices

The UK has a highly educated and skilled workforce. By investing in research and development it can utilise these skills to bring out innovative products. Many Western and luxury brands are highly aspired to around the world. This allows UK businesses to compete, especially in countries such as China where a new middle class have rising standards of living and want luxury UK brands e.g. Burberry.

A skilled workforce and investment in technology also allows the UK to produce high quality products that are desired across the world. Efficiency and quality control make these products highly desirable. Specialisation also means that these goods and services can be produced at a lower cost allowing businesses to charge a lower price.

Burberry is a global luxury brand. In 2018 it had revenues of £2.7bn and an operating profit of £467m. Its biggest target market is countries from the Asia Pacific region, such as China. It has a focus of expanding in key markets, with high levels of consumer income creating demand for luxury goods. It has a highly skilled workforce, with over 10 000 employees around the world. These produce a range of textiles and leather products that are showcased at fashion shows. Burberry is looking to expand its digital and social media content, making it easier to engage with customers around the world.

To what extent does globalisation benefit UK businesses?

Benefits of globalisation to UK businesses	Drawbacks of globalisation to UK businesses
Greater access to foreign markets, e.g. the UK has a world reputation for its financial services. Access to wider markets enables businesses to invest in R&D as product life cycles are longer. The UK can import the goods and services that it needs easily, with less restrictions on trade. The UK can access specialist skills from other countries.	The UK struggles to compete on cost for manufactured goods as wage rates in the UK are relatively high. The UK has suffered structural unemployment based on the loss of some industries that it can no longer compete in based on price. The UK is subject to international laws of trade.

Exchange rates are the price of one currency in terms of another e.g. £1 = $1.15.

An increase in the value of a currency is called an appreciation and means that the currency is worth more e.g. £1 = $1.20. A decrease in the value of a currency is called a depreciation and means that a currency is worth less e.g. £1 = $1.10.

The value of a currency will affect businesses ability to import and export goods and services
- **Imports** are those goods and services that we **buy** from other countries
- **Exports** are those goods and services that we **sell** to other countries

As the £ appreciates, imports become cheaper and exports dearer. This means that the sales and profits of a business that imports will improve whilst those of a business that exports will decline. The opposite is true if the £ depreciates.

SPICED   Strong Pound Imports Cheaper Exports Dearer
WPIDEC   Weak Pound Imports Dearer Exports Cheaper

The weak pound has seen the profits of UK firms impacted in different ways. FTSE 100 companies gain about 70% of sales overseas. As a result, they have benefited from increased sales as the £ has depreciated against the $ in the 2 years to the end of 2018. Burberry, for example, has seen a boost in sales from the US market. However, businesses such as Sports Direct, who buy most of its sportswear from abroad, have been impacted negatively by the decline in the value of the £.

Which UK businesses will benefit most from a fall in the value of the £?

Globalisation has meant increased **competition from overseas** for UK businesses. This comes at the expense of domestic businesses, so demand will fall for UK goods and services. This is particularly the case for low cost imports such as textiles.

However, UK businesses benefit by **buying imports from overseas** and selling them on to UK consumers. This might be in the form of:
- Finished goods
- Semi-manufactured goods
- Raw materials

UK businesses profit by adding value. For example, supermarkets make it easy and convenient to buy foreign produced fruit and vegetables; car manufacturers import components for producing cars in the UK.

UK businesses compete internationally, **selling to overseas markets** by offering:
- Better designs
    - Innovative products
    - Well respected British brands
    - Luxury brands
- Higher quality products
    - High levels of quality control
    - High added value
    - Use of advanced technologies

Changing business locations has seen many UK businesses relocate abroad, particularly for manufacturing. This has led to closing down UK plants to benefit from cheaper resources abroad e.g. labour and raw materials and moving closer to large markets such as China.
- Outsourcing abroad involves closing down UK facilities and using the services of a third party located overseas e.g. call centres based in India. UK businesses can benefit from cheaper resources or more skilled employees
- Inward and outward investment means UK businesses can establish a branch or subsidiary abroad or foreign businesses might locate in the UK. The UK car industry has benefited from this. Despite being the second biggest car producer in Europe there are no large UK owned car manufacturers. This normally means capital investment into the UK e.g. new factories

Multinational businesses are those that operate in more than one country. Many are recognisable global brands. They operate in a number of major global markets, including:
- North America
- European Union
- South-East Asia

There are a number of benefits of being a multinational, including global brand recognition, targeting a wider market, taking advantage of lower production costs and economies of scale such as the ability to buy in bulk.

However, there are also disadvantages. These include communication and coordination problems, differences in culture and legal systems and vulnerability to fluctuations in exchange rates.

Countries may try to stop or reduce the amount of goods or services coming into the country. The actions taken are called barriers to trade. These include tariffs and trading blocs. Barriers to international trade include:

Tariffs: a tax on imports.

This will increase the cost of exporting the product. Therefore, prices will be more expensive, lowering demand. The UK will look to create new deals with non-EU countries upon leaving the EU, trying to lower tariffs with these countries. As a member of the EU it is not allowed to negotiate its own tariffs with other countries. One benefit of being in the EU is that there are no taxes between member states when exporting goods and services.

Trade blocs: when a group of countries join together to reduce barriers to trade.

This makes trade between them easier and cheaper, increasing demand. However, countries outside the trading bloc will face barriers to trade, making it more difficult for businesses to sell their product.

There are a number of trade blocs around the world:
- The UK is a member of the European Union (28 members) until 2019
- NAFTA (North American Free Trade Agreement) is made up of the USA, Canada and Mexico
- ASEAN (Association of South East Asian Nations)

How businesses compete internationally
The use of the internet and e-commerce:

The internet and e-commerce have made communications easier, meaning that buyers and sellers are now interconnected on a global basis. Access to the internet has continued to grow, leading to greater demand from consumers worldwide. This makes it easier to use e-commerce to grow sales and market share. This has led businesses to target markets around the world, thus creating the potential for enormous increases in sales.

Changing the marketing mix to compete internationally:

UK businesses can charge higher prices abroad as they have a reputation for quality. They can access foreign markets, particularly through e-commerce. However, dominant businesses from around the world are accessing the UK, particularly through enhanced technology.

Global advertising creates economies of scale, reducing unit costs. UK businesses will adapt marketing to meet local expectations. UK businesses can buy cheaper imported products and add value in the UK, or resale these goods abroad.

The UK has a highly skilled workforce e.g. financial services, producing quality products. These will need to be adapted for different markets. UK businesses can hire the best employees from around the globe to enhance the quality of their products.

However, foreign businesses, especially from the US, have used their superior marketing power and expertise to dominate markets.

Test Yourself

2.1.3 Business and globalisation

1. What is globalisation?

2. Explain how UK businesses can compete in international markets by producing higher quality goods.

3. State one other way in which UK businesses compete internationally.

4. Explain one advantage of globalisation to UK businesses.

5. Explain one disadvantage of globalisation to UK businesses.

6. What are exchange rates?

7. What are imports?

8. What are exports?

9. Explain the impact of a falling exchange rate on the profit and sales of a business that imports.

10. Explain the impact of a rising exchange rate on the profit and sales of a business that exports.

2.1.4 Ethics, the environment and business

What you need to learn
- The impact of ethical and environmental considerations on businesses:
  - how ethical considerations influence business activity: possible trade-offs between ethics and profit
  - how environmental considerations influence business activity: possible trade-offs between the environment, sustainability and profit
  - the potential impact of pressure group activity on the marketing mix

Ethical and environmental considerations

Social costs and benefits are the costs and benefits to society created by the activities of a business. A business may want to take action to limit its social costs and maximise its social benefits.

Cadbury's Dairy Milk is a **Fairtrade** product. 15 000 tonnes of Fairtrade cocoa are sourced from Ghana, benefitting the producers in this developing country. Cadbury's pay a guaranteed minimum price for the cocoa, even if the market price falls to a lower level. Cadbury's is not alone. The Fairtrade Foundation states that there has been rapid growth in the sales of Fairtrade products.

Business ethics are the moral standards by which business behaviour is judged i.e. whether business activities are considered to be morally right or wrong.

Examples of poor ethics	Examples of good ethics
Exploiting labour	Paying fair wages
Providing false information to customers	Using sustainable materials
Bullying suppliers	Minimising environmental impact
Water, air or noise pollution	Prioritising animal welfare
Destruction of the physical environment	Not exploiting workers
	Considering stakeholders in business decisions

Businesses such as Nestle have faced significant criticism in the way that they source their ingredients. Deforestation and biodiversity loss are destroying the habitats of animals such as the orangutan; human rights abuses are bringing misery to indigenous populations. The lack of sustainable production of products such as palm oil is impacting negatively on the reputation of some multinational corporations.

Can you think of examples of poor or good ethics at businesses that you are familiar with?

A **trade-off** occurs when a range of alternatives is given up to achieve the benefit of something else. For example, if a business behaves ethically it may be giving up the opportunity to maximise profits.

Examples of possible trade-offs between ethics and profit include:

- If a fair price is paid to suppliers in order not to exploit them this will increase costs, therefore reducing profits. However, this may not be true if customers are willing to pay a higher price for ethically sourced goods
- If employees are treated fairly, with a good wage and working conditions, this will increase costs. However, in the long run motivated employees may be more productive and retention rates may be higher, reducing the costs of recruitment and training
- Providing customers with fair prices may lower revenue. However, this may attract more customers, allowing a business to improve market share
- Using environmentally friendly production processes, with low pollution, can increase costs. However, this can help a business avoid fines and build a good reputation amongst customers, leading to more repeat business

Ethical behaviour requires businesses to act in ways that stakeholders consider to be both fair and honest.

Advantages of ethical behaviour	Disadvantages of ethical behaviour
Good reputation leading to brand loyalty and hence repeat business. Able to charge a premium price as customers are willing to pay more for ethical products. Avoid negative publicity that could damage the brand's reputation. Attract top employees who are motivated by working for an ethical business.	Can increase costs leading to a possible loss of competitiveness and profitability. Takes time to write and review ethical policies. Opportunity cost of management time spent ensuring ethical standards are maintained. Difficulty in ensuring ethical standards are maintained throughout the supply chain.

Made for Life Organics sell uncontaminated natural cosmetics products that have not been tested on animals. The business advocates the use of natural ingredients in recycled packaging that has a focus on its carbon footprint. The Made for Life Foundation offers emotional and practical support for those who have suffered from cancer. Over 10 000 people have attended Made for Life support days run by the charity.

To what extent does having an ethical stance benefit a business?

Environmental considerations look at how the activities of businesses and consumers impact on the natural world e.g. plants, animals and air quality.

Environmental considerations	Businesses	Consumers
Traffic congestion	Timings of deliveries to and from stores e.g. off peak. Car share schemes for employees and closer parking for customers who car share. Online ordering and delivery services.	Car share. Use public transport or park and ride to reduce congestion in cities and towns.

Environmental considerations	Businesses	Consumers
Recycling	Providing facilities e.g. recycling bins. Reduced use of packaging. Use of recycling materials within the production process.	Buy refillable products. Recycle waste. Encouraging businesses to reduce their use of packaging. Reusing carrier bags. Favouring environmentally friendly producers.

Environmental considerations	Businesses	Consumers
Disposing of waste	Safe disposal of waste generated in the production process. Finding alternative uses for waste e.g. using waste to feed animals.	Safe disposal of domestic waste. Reducing waste e.g. not buying more food than will be eaten by the household.
Noise and air pollution	Reduce carbon emissions e.g. sourcing supplies locally or electric delivery vans. Safe practices to ensure environmental disasters don't happen.	Reducing carbon footprint e.g. buying from local business and reducing food miles. Low emission cars or alternative methods of transport.

Costs to businesses of accepting environmental responsibilities	Benefits to businesses of accepting environmental responsibilities
Need to carry out "green" or environmental audits. Time spent writing and reviewing environmental policies. Possible trade-off with profit. Cost of implementing environmentally friendly machinery, filters or processes.	Good reputation attracting environmentally conscious consumers. Reduced waste in operations. Avoiding negative media attention through campaigns by pressure groups. No expensive clean-up operations following a disaster or fines. Easier to attract investors and employees. Personal peace of mind for business owners.

Environmental **sustainability** considers how a business uses its resources and if it is replanting and renewing these resources fast enough to ensure that its stocks do not deplete.

Sustainability is important in supporting long-term development. The use of unsustainable practices will lead to irreversible damage to the environment having a negative effect on the quality of life of future generations.

Two major issues of sustainability are:

Global warming is a rise in the Earth's temperature. It is caused by greenhouse gases produced by human activities. These include deforestation and the use of fossil fuels. In 80 years' time the world is expected to be 6 degrees warmer than it is now. Business will be affected through legislation and opportunities for new products. Global warming will also impact on the availability of resources for a business.

Resource depletion is caused as we use up **scarce resources** such as petrol and coal. With decreasing supply and increasing demand, as the world has become richer, prices have risen dramatically. Greater emphasis has been placed on using renewable resources such as solar power and wind energy.

There can be a trade-off between sustainability and profit. This means that a business may sacrifice or give up some profit in order to behave ethically. For example, a business that uses renewable resources may experience higher costs. This could result in lower profits. However, this may not be true if customers are willing to pay a higher price for sustainably produced goods and services.

A ban on plastic straws could be introduced in the UK. Sometimes businesses need to be forced, by the Government, to take environmentally responsible decisions. In recent years this has included the introduction of a 5p charge on plastic bags. In 2018 the Prime Minster, Theresa May, said that plastic waste was one of the biggest environmental concerns. It is estimated that 8.9 billion plastic straws are thrown away every year in the UK alone. Legislation may be introduced to ban the use of these. Paper Straw Co, based in Manchester, is the first British business to make paper straws in this country for decades. However, paper straws can cost up to three times as much as plastic straws to make.

The potential impact of pressure group activity on the marketing mix

Pressure groups are people with a common cause or interest. They act collectively to create public awareness and try to change the behaviour of business, consumers and government. Examples of pressure groups in the UK include Amnesty International, Greenpeace, Shelter and trade unions. Consumers can influence business behaviour through membership of pressure groups.

Price	Product
Costs are likely to increase so businesses will pass this on to the consumer in the form of higher prices. Consumers are more willing to pay higher prices for ethical products.	Businesses will produce ethical products that meet the needs of the consumer, increasing their reputation. Products might be removed from the product range or have ingredients/raw materials changed. Businesses will improve relationships with key stakeholders such as suppliers and employees.
Promotion	**Place**
Businesses can use their improved reputation to promote their products. They will consider the medium that that they use to market their products, to see if these are appropriate in order to meet the demands of their stakeholders e.g. customers.	Businesses will have to consider where they can open new stores. They will source products from local areas to support the community and reduce damage to the environment.

Test Yourself

2.1.4 Ethics, the environment and business

1. What are ethical considerations?

2. What are trade-offs?

3. Explain why there may be a trade-off between ethics and profit.

4. Give two examples of ethical behaviour of businesses to customers.

5. Give two examples of ethical behaviour of businesses to suppliers.

6. State two examples of environmental considerations.

7. What is sustainability?

8. Explain why there may be a trade-off between sustainability and profit.

9. State one advantage and one disadvantage of ethical behaviour.

10. Explain one potential impact of pressure group activity on the following elements of the marketing mix:
    a. Price
    b. Product
    c. Promotion
    d. Place

2.2.1 Product

> **What you need to learn**
> - The design mix:
>   - function, aesthetics, cost.
> - The product life cycle:
>   - the phases of the product life cycle
>   - extension strategies
> - The importance to a business of differentiating a product/ service

Product is the **goods** and **services** that a business provides.

Design mix is the three fundamental elements of good or service design that must be taken into account during the research and development stage of a new product i.e. prior to launching onto the market.

Function	Aesthetics	Cost
The purpose of the product i.e. what is actually does. This may include additional features.	The appearance of the product. This can include its attractiveness to the eye as well as how it feels or smells.	The ability to produce the product at a reasonable price. This assesses the economic feasibility of the product.

A **product life cycle** shows the sales of a product over time. There are five stages associated with the product life cycle:

Research and development - before the product has been launched onto the market
- Sales are zero and the product is therefore not contributing to revenue
- Spending on research and development is likely to be high

Introduction - the product is launched onto the market
- Likely to be expensive as the firm advertises in order to raise awareness
- Sales could be slow to start which could lead to initial losses
- Launch can see immediate high sales if the product has been promoted heavily in advance to create hype e.g. when Apple launch a new phone

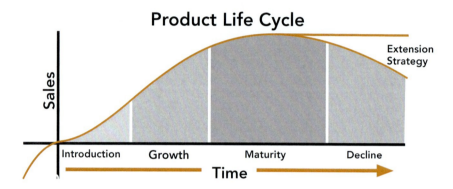

Growth - sales start to increase
- Consumers become familiar with the product and repeat custom is built up
- No longer needs to be promoted so heavily
- May start to make a profit as costs are lower and revenues rising

Maturity - sales reach a peak and start to level off
- Competition may become stronger
- The business will still spend money on promoting the product to try and maintain customer's interest and prolong this stage for as long as possible
- The product should now be contributing to the business' profits

Decline - sales start to fall
- The firm will decide on either an extension strategy or discontinuing the product

A business may use **extension strategies** to extend the life of the product. These are used when a product reaches maturity in order to try and extend its period of maturity and stop it going into decline. Extension strategies may include:
- updating packaging
- adding more or different features
- changing target market
- advertising
- price reduction

These may be supported with a new promotional campaign.

Extension strategies will impact on other aspects of the business:
- Operations management - research and development is required
- Finance - increased costs for product development and promotion
- Marketing - the 4Ps will need to be considered
- People - has the business the human resource skills required to develop the product?

A business with a balanced portfolio will have products at different stages of the life cycle. This allows it to use profits from mature products to support new products during the development and launch stages.

A product portfolio is the range of products that a business sells. As a firm expands it is likely to offer more products to:
- Broaden its product range
  - Different target markets for similar products
  - New product development
- Balance their product range
  - Offer a range of goods or services to support the original products
  - Meet the needs of different customers

Both of these actions help a business to grow and spread risk. If one market is in decline other markets may be growing.

A business might have a **product range** selling a variety of goods or services to meet consumer needs. With high competition in most markets it is important that a business tries to differentiate itself from the competition in order to maximise sales.

In order to make a product stand out from competitors a business may have a **unique selling point** (USP). This is something that distinguishes a business' product from those of its competitors. This could be a design feature, a product feature or a distinctive image. It provides a competitive advantage.

A USP is significant in a competitive market:
- A business needs a USP to differentiate its products from competitors. If it doesn't have one it would have to compete on price
- In some markets, with some customers, price is the most important element of the marketing mix. A business should research its market to see what USP is desirable

Businesses try to make their product different to the competition by adapting the actual product in some way or by distinguishing the product through advertising and branding.

Creating a **brand image** is a promotional method that involves the creation of an identity for the business that distinguishes the business and its products from competitors. Branding can add value to a product allowing businesses to charge higher prices. This leads to brand loyalty whereby customers will continue to buy products from that business. A good brand image is important in a competitive market.

Test Yourself

2.2.1 Product

1. What is a product?

2. Explain one reason why function must be taken into account when designing a good or service.

3. Explain one reason why aesthetics must be taken into account when designing a good or service.

4. Explain one reason why cost must be taken into account when designing a good or service.

5. What is a product life cycle?

6. With reference to the product life cycle explain how demand for a product changes over time.

7. What is the relationship between the stages of the product life cycle and the ability of a product to generate profit?

8. Explain two methods a business may use to extend the life of a product.

9. State two benefits to a business of having a range of products.

10. Distinguish between a unique selling point and brand image.

2.2.2 Price

> **What you need to learn**
> - Price
>   - pricing strategies
>   - influences on pricing strategies: technology, competition, market segments, product life cycle

Price

The amount of **money** a customer will have to **pay** for the good being sold or service provided.

The price charged will depend on a number of factors including:
- Market research findings
- Price charged by competitors
- Costs to the business
- The state of the economy i.e. how much money customers have

In a competitive market there is normally a clear relationship between price and demand i.e. the quantity sold.
- As price goes ↑ demand goes ↓
- As price goes ↓ demand goes ↑

If there is a lot of competition in the market it is harder for a business to raise its price as customers might go elsewhere and revenue will fall. If there is a lack of competition the business might have the opportunity to raise its prices and increase revenue.

Business can choose to charge either a high price or a low price. This might be linked to the quality of the product.

There are a variety of pricing methods used by a business when trying to grow. Remember there is a close link between price and demand.

When launching a new product a business will often choose between price skimming and price penetration.

Price skimming	Price penetration
Setting a high price at the launch of a product as some consumers are willing to pay a high price for the product to have it immediately.	Setting a low price in order to gain market share.
Using this method means that a business maximises revenues at the high end of the market, normally those with higher disposable incomes.	Once this objective has been met and customers like the product the business will raise prices.
Once the top end of the market has been 'skimmed' the business will lower prices.	The idea is to build up a customer base and hope for repeat custom once prices have been increased.
Frequently used with new technological products as it helps quickly recover some of the research and development costs.	This tends to be used when the business is targeting a mass market.

Business will also use various pricing methods to try and influence the demand for established products. These include:

- **Competitive pricing**
    - A business will have to take into account the prices of other businesses in the market
    - The greater the degree of competition in the market the more important price becomes
    - Prices will be closely linked to those of competitors when there are lots of identical or nearly identical products available e.g. milk
- **Loss leader**
    - A business sets price below the cost of the product and therefore makes a loss on that product
    - This can attract customers to a store where they will also buy additional products
    - Some firms sell the core product as a loss leader and make additional sales by selling accessories to the product e.g. a free app but you then buy additional features
- **Cost-plus**
    - A business sets a price based on the unit cost of making the product plus a percentage mark up
    - This ensures that every unit sold at least covers the total cost of the product

In the exam you will not be asked about specific pricing strategies. However, an understanding of these may help you write more theoretical answers to impress the examiner.

Cost-plus example:

Theo builds garden furniture. The unit cost of making one shed is £65. He uses cost-plus pricing and adds a 30% mark-up.

Cost	£65.00
Mark-up	£19.50 Workings (£65.00/100 x 30 = **£19.50**)
Selling price	£84.50

There are a number of influences on pricing strategies. These include:

Technology

New technology can help bring down the cost of producing a product but can be expensive initially. As the process of making the product changes a business can choose to:
- Change price
- Experience a change in profits. If costs go up and prices stay the same profit margins will fall

New technological products can add value:
- Early adopters are willing to pay more for the product
- Product life cycles might be shorter
- A business can reduce prices to increase sales, whilst bringing out a new version of the product as an extension strategy

Competition
- Competition tends to push prices down
- Fewer businesses mean less competition therefore businesses will tend to compete on factors other than price e.g. promotion
- The internet and new technology have increased the degree of competition in many markets leading to lower, more competitive pricing

Market segments
- Targeting specific sections of the market will impact on the price charged
- Who the customer is and what are they willing to pay for the product is clearly important. This will depend on disposable income
- Brand image is important in allowing businesses to charge higher prices
- In a mass market prices may be lower than in a small specialist market i.e. a niche
- Prices will also be influenced by the nature of the product e.g. a luxury or a necessity. This will depend on the target market

The product life cycle
- A business will take into account where its products are on the product life cycle
- New products might be set at a premium price in order to skim the market; alternatively they could be set at a low price to establish a foothold in the market
- Mature products might act as cash cows and be set at a standard price
- Products in decline might see a fall in price as there is less demand for them

Test Yourself

2.2.2 Price

1. Explain the difference between price skimming and price penetration.

2. What is meant by competitive pricing?

3. What is meant by loss leader pricing?

4. What is meant by cost-plus pricing?

5. Walter owns a removal business. He has total fixed costs of £20 000 and variable costs of £100 per day. He works 250 days per year. Walter uses a cost-plus pricing method with a mark-up of 50%. How much does Walter charge for one day's work?

6. Explain a suitable pricing method for a business looking to enter a competitive market.

7. Explain why new technology can influence pricing strategies.

8. Explain why the level of competition can influence pricing strategies.

9. Explain why the type of market segment targeted can influence pricing strategies.

10. Explain why the position on the product life cycle can influence pricing strategies.

2.2.3 Promotion

What you need to learn
- Promotion:
  - appropriate promotion strategies for different market segments: advertising, sponsorship, product trials, special offers, branding
  - the use of technology in promotion: targeted advertising online, viral advertising via social media, e-newsletters

Promotion is all of the activities designed to increase awareness, interest in and sales of a product.

Promotional methods are the way in which a business informs or persuades target markets to buy its products.

Advertising is communication used to inform potential customers about products and persuade them to buy the products.

Advertising takes a variety of forms including:
- newspapers and magazines
- television
- internet
- billboards

As businesses grow they can afford to pay for more expensive advertising that will reach a wider market. This will lead to an increase in the potential customer base and if successful higher sales revenue.

Sponsorship is when a business gives financial support to an event in return for high profile exposure of the business' brand name.
Sponsorship can target a variety of areas including:
- Cultural
- Sporting
- Musical

Sponsorship of events can gain nationwide or even global publicity for a business. This awareness can enable the business to expand into national or global markets.

Product trials are a method of raising awareness of a product, normally before a national launch, by allowing consumers early access to it.

The product can be trialled in specific areas before being rolled out nationally.

If the trial is successful the business might take the next step, fully launching the product with a range of promotional strategies.

Special offers are a short-term method of promotion designed to attract customers to purchase a product. They can take a variety of forms, including:
- Point of sale displays
- 2 for 1 offers
- Free gifts
- Samples
- Coupons
- Competitions

As they grow businesses target a wider audience through national special offers.

Branding is a promotional method that involves the creation of an identity for the business that distinguishes it and its products from other businesses. This can add value to a product allowing firms to charge higher prices. It leads to brand loyalty whereby customers will continue to buy products from that business.

Established business such as Apple can use their brand name, image and reputation to help in product trials. Consumers are likely to be repeat purchasers of branded products as they believe in the quality of the good or service.

The use of technology in promotion:

Targeted advertising online

Websites gather information regarding internet use by potential customers. Cookies make this easier for businesses to do.

A cookie is a piece of data that is sent from a website that an internet user has visited. This is stored in your browser. When you return to that website your computer will send information back to the site, which will tailor what is shown to you based on your prior search. This allows businesses to tailor advertising based on your personal preferences. The more we use a site, the more a business knows about us. This allows businesses to send targeted advertising. This might occur at the time we visit a web page or it could be any time that we access the internet.

Viral advertising via social media

This is the use of social media to encourage the spread of promotional activities and increase brand awareness. Businesses will launch a form of marketing communication such as a blog, video clip, promotional vouchers or games using social media. This helps to establish awareness through online word of mouth as recipients share the communication with their own networks. Hence the communication is spread like a virus. This is:

- Quick, cheap and easy to do
- Supported by a range of other promotional methods
- Only one part of the process to increase revenues

Popular mediums for viral marketing include Facebook, twitter and YouTube.

E-newsletters

These are bulletins that are sent out to subscribers at regular intervals. This may be daily, weekly, monthly or intermittently. Content will vary with each newsletter sent out.

Businesses can provide information about a wide variety of topics, building awareness of the brand and the product range. This helps establish the business as an expert or authority in their specific area. Popular e-newsletters can carry advertising as a way of driving revenues.

Test Yourself

2.2.3 Promotion

1. Identify two forms of advertising.

2. Explain how a business can use advertising to achieve growth.

3. What is sponsorship?

4. Explain one benefit of carrying out product trials to a business.

5. Identify three types of special offers.

6. Explain one benefit of special offers to a business.

7. Explain one benefit of branding to a business.

8. Explain why targeted online advertising can increase the customer base of a business.

9. Explain why viral advertising can rapidly increase demand for a product.

10. Explain one reason why e-newsletters can be beneficial to a business.

2.2.4 Place

What you need to learn
- Place:
  - methods of distribution: retailers and e-tailers (e-commerce)

Place refers to both the route a product takes from the producer to the end customer as well as the location where a customer can obtain a product.

The route a product takes from the producer to the end customer is called the **channel of distribution**. This can be **direct** or via a number of **intermediaries** e.g. retailers or wholesalers.

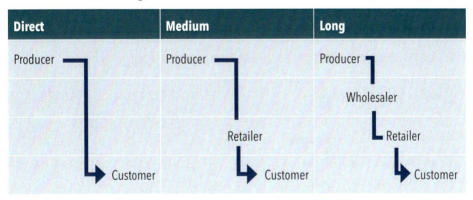

There are two main **intermediaries** i.e. other businesses a product can pass through from producer to customer.

Retailers
- A business that buys from a manufacturer or wholesaler and sells on to the general public
- Large retailers can hold a great deal of power over their suppliers negotiating substantial discounts
- Retailers make the products readily available to customers

Wholesalers
- A business that provides a link between the producer of goods and the retailer
- They buy large quantities of goods and break these down to sell to retailers in smaller amounts e.g. a wholesaler may buy a pallet containing 1200 bottles of water but sell to retailers in boxes of 24
- The wholesaler will gain a discount for bulk buying and add on a percentage as their profit before selling on to retailers

Telesales
- This is a method of direct marketing, usually over the telephone, but also through other face to face media such as web conferencing
- As firms grow they often make use of call centres to 'cold call' people nationwide
- Although this can lead to a poor reputation it can also increase sales revenue

E-tailers (e-commerce), or electronic commerce, is when buyers and sellers meet in a virtual location i.e. the internet.

M-commerce, or mobile commerce, is the use of mobile devices such as smart phones or tablets to trade.

Both of these allow for retailing to take place 24/7. They reduce geographical restrictions, allowing a customer to have greater choice and a business a wider target market, including international markets. There is added convenience for customers, who can choose from home delivery or click and collect. Finally, these can help a business avoid high costs associated with retail premises.

Test Yourself

2.2.4 Place

1. What is meant by the term place?

2. Explain one disadvantage of using a retailer to distribute a product.

3. Explain one advantage of using a retailer to distribute a product.

4. Why might a business try to reach customers directly rather than through a number of intermediaries?

5. Explain two benefits to a business of internet selling.

6. Distinguish between e-commerce and m-commerce.

7. Identify one benefit of e-commerce.

8. Identify one drawback of m-commerce.

9. Identify one disadvantage of e-retailers.

10. Explain one way that e-tailers can meet the needs of customers.

2.2.5 Using the marketing mix to make business decisions

> **What you need to learn**
> - How each element of the marketing mix can influence other elements
> - Using the marketing mix to build competitive advantage
> - How an integrated marketing mix can influence competitive advantage

When choosing a marketing mix a business should consider:
- The target market
- The nature of the competition
- The actions of the competitors
- The type of product
- Where the product is in the product life cycle
- The level of differentiation that can be achieved
- The brand name and reputation of the business
- The business' objectives

How each element of the marketing mix can influence other elements

A high-quality **product**
- Will tend to have a premium price
- Will be promoted through notable, perhaps niche, publications
- Will be distributed through renowned outlets

A low-cost **product**
- Will tend to have a low price
- Will be promoted through mass media
- Will be distributed through mass outlets

A high quality product	A low-cost product
Burberry charge over £1000 for one of their famous jackets. They advertise their clothes in magazines such as Vogue. They are sold in Burberry's own designer stores or other famous retail outlets such as Harrods.	Greggs charge £2 for sausage/bacon in a bun and a hot drink. They advertise their food through a range of mass media such as television. They are sold in stores across the country that are easily accessible by a large number of customers.

Using the marketing mix to build competitive advantage

Business will use the marketing mix to inform and implement business decisions:

- Product portfolio – need for new products or to delete products based on the stage in the product life cycle
- Pricing decisions based on objectives and competitors' actions
- Promotional activities and technological or social change
- Place e.g. growth of e-commerce and m-commerce

It is important for a business' marketing mix to evolve over time based on both internal and external changes. This is required to help maintain a competitive advantage. A competitive advantage is a feature of a business that makes it more attractive to customers than its rivals. This may be based on a wide range of factors affecting the customers' perceptions including price, convenience and quality.

How an integrated marketing mix can influence competitive advantage

If a business integrates its marketing mix successfully it will achieve a competitive advantage. A high-priced low-quality product is doomed to failure once consumers realise that they are not getting value for money. A low-priced high-quality product is doomed to failure once businesses realise that they are making a loss on selling each product.

Advertising a premium product e.g. a Bentley car in a mass media publication e.g. the Sun newspaper is ineffective as the vast majority of readers cannot afford to buy it. Far better to target readers of the Financial Times.

Clearly, getting the right mix is going to make a business more competitive in the market in which it operates.

The marketing mix at Kurt Geiger - *Over 500 million pairs of shoes are sold in the UK every year. The market is worth over £5 billion. Kurt Gieger has positioned itself as a high quality product within this market. By concentrating on design it has managed to gain a loyal following for its shoes and are able to charge a premium (high) price. An important element of its success is how it manages to sell its shoes in top department stores around the country alongside its own prestigious shoe shops. To enhance its image it advertises in high end magazines such as Marie Claire.*

Test Yourself

2.2.5 Using the marketing mix to make business decisions

1. What is meant by an integrated marketing mix?

2. What is meant by a competitive advantage?

3. Explain how price can affect promotion.

4. Explain how product can affect price.

5. Explain how promotion can affect product.

6. Explain how an integrated marketing mix can help a business to build a competitive advantage.

7. Explain one possible method of distribution for a business selling high-quality products.

8. Explain one possible method of distribution for a business selling low-cost products.

9. Explain one possible method of promotion for a business selling high-quality products.

10. Explain one possible method of promotion for a business selling high-quality products.

2.3.1 Business operations

What you need to learn
- The purpose of business operations:
  - to produce goods
  - to provide services
- Production processes:
  - different types: job, batch, flow
  - the impact of different types of production process: keeping productivity up and costs down and allowing for competitive prices
- Impacts of technology on production:
  - balancing cost, productivity, quality and flexibility

Business operations is the management and coordination of resources to create a good or service.
Goods are tangible products i.e. they can be touched
- Businesses transform raw materials into finished goods
- Examples include cars and computers

Services are intangible products i.e. they cannot be touched
- Businesses use their resources, skills and experience to provide a service
- Examples include banking and teaching

Methods of production include:
Job production
The production of one off items to meet the needs of each individual customer.
- Cheap and easy to set up, but more expensive to produce
- Often a specialist service
- Time consuming to produce
- Meet specific needs of customers
- Examples include:
  - Tailor made clothes and jewellery
  - Specialist cakes
  - Web designs

Delicious chocolates for that special moment - *Natalie Allen founded Delicious Moments as she saw a gap in the market for a bespoke chocolate service. She produces a range of chocolates that can be customised according to customer tastes. Customers can order their own shapes, chocolate, fillings and even colours to match their special event such as weddings. The tailor made chocolates are produced using job production. Once Natalie has her customer's requirements she sets about producing outstanding chocolates tailored to the event. People are willing to pay high prices for this sort of premium product meaning that Delicious Moments can compete against lower priced, lower quality offerings.*

Job production	
Advantages	**Disadvantages**
• Low cost to set up initially as expensive machinery or large amounts of stock is probably not needed • Products can be tailor made to suit individual needs • A premium price can be charged • Care is usually taken over each item, resulting in high quality • Allows a business to differentiate itself from competitors	• Difficult to achieve economies of scale, therefore unit costs may be high • Often requires skilled labour, increasing costs • Time consuming to produce, so output may be low • Goods are expensive, which may limit the market • Output will be limited, which may make it difficult to meet demand

Batch Production

Identical items are produced in groups (batches), each item passing through the production process at the same time.
- Allows for cheaper and quicker production of individual items
- More uniform products
- Variation can be achieved in different batches
- Examples include:
  - Bread
  - Jeans
  - Garden furniture

Batch production	
Advantages	**Disadvantages**
<ul><li>Cheaper to produce an entire batch</li><li>Lower wage costs as often made by machines</li><li>Less waste and faulty products as machines are more efficient</li><li>Can produce a range of similar products using the same machinery</li></ul>	<ul><li>Downtime (known as cycle time) as machinery is changed from one batch to another, leading to lower productivity</li><li>Expensive to store inventory</li><li>Machinery can break down, meaning there is no production</li></ul>

Flow production

- Items flow along the production line in a continuous process
- Suitable for mass production
    - Large scale
    - Identical items
- Uses specialist machinery
- Workers are each responsible for a small step along the process, this involves:
    - Specialisation
    - Division of labour

Greggs the Baker has ten regional bakeries. These deliver on a daily basis to 1 641 shops. They employ 20 000 people and have continued to expand across the UK. This expansion has led to plans for the building of a new £35m savoury manufacturing plant in the south of England.

The impact of different types of production process: keeping productivity up and costs down and allowing for competitive prices

Productivity can be defined as output per worker. A business would look at productivity over a period of time e.g. one year and compare it with previous years. Technology, such as machinery, speeds up the production process and increases the quantity made per worker.

A business will set targets linked to keeping unit costs as low as possible whilst not affecting quality.

Technology influences unit costs		
Increased number of units produced	**Productivity**	**Material usage**
• Spreads fixed costs • Negotiate discounts with suppliers through bulk buying • Greater use of assets	• Efficiency of workforce • Use of workforce hours	• Reduces wastage

A business can pass reduced costs onto the consumer through lower prices. This is particularly important in competitive markets when a customer can go elsewhere. Alternatively, the business might maintain its prices, meaning that lower costs can lead to higher profit margins for every unit sold.

Impact of technology on production: balancing cost, productivity, quality and flexibility

- Increased competitiveness
  - Ability to reach global markets
  - E-commerce
  - Greater productivity and consistency/quality
  - Lower unit costs and less waste
- Move from labour to capital intensive
  - Redundancies
  - Retraining
  - Cost
  - Initially expensive to pay for new technology
  - However, reduces unit costs in the long run
- Productivity
  - Increased output per worker
  - Higher capacity
- Quality
  - Increased consistency with less waste
  - Improved quality without human error
- Flexibility
  - Ability to change products being produced
  - A range of products can be made on same machinery

Test Yourself

2.3.1 Business operations

1. What are business operations?

2. What is job production?

3. State one type of good where job production is appropriate.

4. Explain one advantage and one disadvantage of job production.

5. What is batch production?

6. Explain one advantage and one disadvantage of batch production.

7. What is flow production?

8. State one type of good where flow production is appropriate.

9. Explain one advantage and one disadvantage of flow production.

10. Explain one impact of technology on production.

2.3.2 Working with suppliers

What you need to learn
- Managing stock:
  - interpretation of bar gate stock graphs
  - the use of just in time (JIT) stock control
- The role of procurement:
  - relationships with suppliers: quality, delivery (cost, speed, reliability), availability, cost, trust
  - the impact of logistics and supply decisions on: costs, reputation, customer satisfaction

Managing stock

Stock is held by businesses to help meet customers' needs. It can be held in 3 forms.

Raw materials	Work in progress	Finished products
e.g. ingredients	e.g. a batch of dough	e.g. a loaf of bread

Raw materials are held to ensure products can be made; finished products can be used to fill differences between output and demand.

Bar gate stock graphs

A management tool used to control and monitor the flow of stock. It shows:
- Lead time
  - The time it takes between placing an order and receiving delivery
  - Lead time can be measured on the horizontal axis of a stock control diagram as the distance from re-order level to minimum stock level

- Re-order level
    - The level of stock which triggers an order. This may be done automatically by a computerised system
- Buffer level of stock
    - Stock held by a business to cope with unforeseen circumstances e.g. sudden increases in demand or break down in supplies
    - When a business reaches its minimum stock level it is left just with buffer stock
- Re-order quantities
    - The point at which an order for new stock is placed. This will be dependent on buffer level of stock and lead time

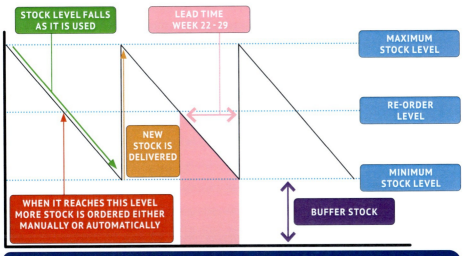

Lead time = delivery date - date of order
e.g. Week 29 - week 22 = 7 weeks

Advantages of holding buffer stock	Disadvantages of holding buffer stock
• Can meet customer demand • Quickly respond to increases in demand • Continue with production even if a problem with stock deliveries	• Money is tied up in holding stock • Costs associated with stock holding e.g. storage, staff, insurance • Risk of waste e.g. out of date, damaged or obsolete

Managing stock involves ensuring that there is enough raw materials and finished goods to meet the demand of the customer. However, for this to be an efficient process a business will want to avoid holding too much stock, which is a cost to a business.

Just in time stock control

A method of stock control where a business aims to reduce waste by ordering stock only when it needs it.

This means that there is no unused or obsolete stock and storage costs are reduced. It also means that less money is tied up in stock.

One major benefit of JIT is reduced costs. This is due to:
- Storage and warehousing are not needed, therefore there is not the associated costs of rent, shelfing, staff and heat and light
- Stock control costs are reduced; for example, there is no need to pay staff to monitor or count stock, or to move it around the premises
- No insurance costs to protect the business against stock that is damaged or destroyed e.g. in a warehouse fire
- Obsolete or damaged stock will be reduced

However, these cost savings need to be balanced against:
- The cost of more frequent deliveries; for example, staff wages for handling stock during deliveries, or transport and administrative costs
- Loss of purchasing economies of scale; for example, loss of discounts offered by suppliers for buying in bulk

In the summer of 2018 several UK manufacturing companies were hit by a shortage in CO2. This included fizzy drink and meat businesses. One producer hit by the shortage was Warburton's, who ran out of carbon dioxide. It uses this when packaging its crumpets, to make them last longer when on the shelves at supermarkets. Warburton's, the largest producer of crumpets in the UK, was forced to stop production in 2 of its 4 factories.

The role of procurement

Procurement is the finding of, purchasing of, or acquisition of goods and services.

Suppliers are those people who are responsible for providing those goods and services to businesses. Regardless of the nature of the business they will have goods and services provided to them from other businesses. Most businesses will work with suppliers.

When a business chooses its suppliers it should set out criteria for the selection process, identifying what are the most important factors for them. This would usually include:

Quality	Delivery, Availability, Trust	Cost
Whether the goods or services are of the correct standard and of a consistent standard. This will have a direct impact upon the level of customer satisfaction, the business' ability to meet legal requirements and its reputation.	The ability of the supplier to deliver the right quantity and quality of goods or services on time. This will have a direct impact on whether a business feels the need to have buffer stock if it fears that suppliers may not be reliable.	How much the business has to pay for the goods or services. This will have a direct impact on the costs to the business and therefore how much they will charge customers, the ability to make a profit and competitiveness.
When choosing a supplier the quality will usually have a direct effect upon the quality of the finished product. The need for quality may also have a direct impact on the operational efficiency of a business. If goods have to be scrapped and remade, especially if a JIT method of stock control is used, this will seriously impact on efficiency.	A business must consider if it is able to make enough of a good to meet demand, if not customer numbers may fall. The reliability of the supplier will reduce the need for a business to have several suppliers in case one lets them down. This will allow the businesses to develop a good working relationship.	This is an important factor for many businesses, especially those who compete on price. A low cost supplier means that a business can charge a lower price or choose to enjoy higher profit margins. Businesses must be careful that low price does not mean substandard quality as value for money is important.

Different businesses will rank the factors in different orders according to which ones best fit with their objectives.

Logistics is the coordination of resources to complete a complex operation.

In terms of business operations procurement and logistics includes getting the raw materials and components into the business in time and then the finished product to the customer e.g. delivered from a warehouse to a retailer on time.

The impact of logistics and supply decisions
- Suppliers will affect unit costs in the following ways:
    - The price of the components directly affects the cost of a product
    - Discounts may be offered for buying in bulk
    - Appropriate payment terms will help businesses avoid bank charges
    - If a supplier can deliver reliably and regularly then stock holding costs can be reduced

- Suppliers will have a direct influence on prices as:
    - High quality components allows businesses to charge a higher price
    - Reliability and speed of supply can add value to a product and allow a premium price to be charged
    - Reliability and quality will help a business establish a good reputation

- Suppliers will affect reputation and customer satisfaction:
    - Quality of raw materials entering the production process
    - Delivery of supplies on time
    - Flexibility to match supply to demand
    - Speed of delivery

Test Yourself

2.3.2 Working with suppliers

1. What are the three forms of stock that a business can hold?

2. What is meant by lead time?

3. What is meant by re-order level?

4. What is meant by buffer stock?

5. Explain one advantage of holding buffer stock.

6. Explain one disadvantage of holding buffer stock.

7. Explain how JIT can be used to manage stock.

8. What is procurement?

9. What is logistics?

10. Explain one way in which supply decisions impact on a business.

2.3.3 Managing quality

What you need to learn
- The concept of quality and its importance in:
  - the production of goods and the provision of services: quality control and quality assurance
  - allowing a business to control costs and gain a competitive advantage

Quality is the ability of a good or service to meet or exceed customers' expectations.

Customers want a good or service that will meet their requirements each and every time. Therefore, consistent quality is important. This will earn customer loyalty and repeat custom. Delivering quality is about meeting the minimum standard that a customer expects for a given good or service. However, the quality expected from a good or service will vary from product to product and between customers.

Customers expect a good or service to meet certain standards. This will include:
- Is it fit for the purpose that it was bought for?
- Does it at least meet minimum standards expected by customers?
- Does the customer believe that the product is worth the money paid?

Quality is important to a business because it:
- Helps build a reputation and gain customer loyalty
- Reduces complaints and returns
- Reduces waste from scrapping faulty products
- Gains positive word of mouth advertising e.g. customers tell a friend

Customers' expectations in terms of quality in the:	
Production of goods	**Provision of services**
Consistent standard.	Suitably qualified staff.
Meets health and safety standards.	Knowledge of the product.
Accurate product information e.g. ingredients in a frozen meal.	Trusted information e.g. advice on a mortgage.
	After sales service.
Fit for purpose i.e. it does what it says it will.	Communication skills.
Meets ethical standards.	

The concept of quality

Businesses must be able to identify and measure quality problems.
Methods of doing this include:
- Customer feedback e.g. satisfaction surveys
- Inspection prior to leaving the factory
- Inspection throughout the production process
- Number of complaints or returns
- Ratings on 3rd party websites e.g. Trip Advisor
- Retention rates or levels of repeat customers

Consequences of quality issues include:
- The cost of scrapping or reworking faulty goods
- The cost of product recalls
- Damage to the value of the brand leading to a fall in brand loyalty
- Bad publicity or word of mouth
- Loss of market share
- Fines for faulty goods
- Poor employee motivation; this can be especially true if employees are constantly handling customer complaints

Public confidence in EU labelling and quality control has been hit by a rash of stories regarding the meat that goes into our food. Details have emerged about a supply chain that has allowed horsemeat to be sold as beef in a range of foods such as Tesco burgers and Findus lasagne. However, it is not all bad news for retailers. Growth has been seen for some businesses, such as smaller farms, that sell direct to the public and have a reputation for maintaining high quality standards.

The production of goods and the provision of services

- **Quality control**
    - Checking/inspecting quality at the end of the production process
    - Quality is the responsibility of a specialist at the end of the process

- **Quality assurance**
    - Checking/inspecting quality at each stage of the production process
    - Quality is the responsibility of everyone throughout the process
    - Achieved through a system of total quality management
    - Making everyone in a business responsible for quality
    - Each employee treats the next person as if they are a customer and ensures that what they pass on to them is of the correct quality

	Quality control	**Quality assurance**
Advantages	Inspection is carried out by a specialist. Reduces the risk of a faulty product reaching the customer. Problem areas can be identified and action taken.	Motivated staff as everyone is given responsibility. Focus on quality throughout the process. Less waste from reworking or scrapping faulty goods. Better reputation due to quality products.
Disadvantages	Waste levels can be high as a fault will only be found at the end of the process. Requires specialist personnel. Operatives may feel demotivated as they are "being checked up on".	Relies on commitment of all staff. Training must be provided. Productivity can be reduced.

Allowing a business to control costs and gain a competitive advantage

- Can help achieve lower unit costs
  - Less waste
  - Higher productivity
- Additional sales
  - Repeat custom
  - Word of mouth advertising
  - Brand loyalty
  - Improved customer satisfaction

Test Yourself

2.3.3 Managing quality

1. What is a quality product?

2. State one expectation of customers in terms of the production of a quality good.

3. State one expectation of customers in terms of the provision of a quality service.

4. Explain one consequence of quality issues.

5. What is quality control?

6. What is quality assurance?

7. Explain one advantage of quality control.

8. Explain one advantage of quality assurance.

9. Explain why maintaining quality can help a business control costs.

10. Explain why maintaining quality can help a business gain a competitive advantage.

2.3.4 The sales process

What you need to learn
- The sales process:
  - product knowledge, speed and efficiency of service, customer engagement, responses to customer feedback, post-sales service
- The importance to businesses of providing good customer service

Customer service is the meeting of customer expectations before, during and after purchasing a good or service.

- For a business it is essential to have good customer service in order to:
  - Distinguish the product from the competition
  - Obtain repeat custom
  - Gain a good reputation

- It is important to provide good customer service in a number of areas:
  - Reliability
  - Product information
  - After sales service

The **sales process** is the steps that take place between a business e.g. a sales assistant or sales person and the customer. This is from initial communication to securing a purchase and providing after sales support.

How would you prefer to receive customer help:
• in person • over the phone • online?

Methods of providing good customer service include:

Product knowledge	To obtain the full benefit of a product the customer needs to know how it works. Expert knowledge of how a product works will allow the business to inform customers when making a sale. Good customer service, based on product information, can make the difference between making and losing a sale. Knowledge should include: • Functions and features • Price • Availability • Comparisons with other products • Additional information e.g. warranties, returns policies, care or installation instructions
Speed and efficiency of service	Customers are busy people and it is easier to shop around using e-commerce. Therefore, it is important that they can access the product as quickly as possible, without any problems. This requires a good relationship with suppliers so that products can be delivered on time. Stores will need to ensure that they have enough stock and service sector businesses enough qualified staff to meet demand. The process will need to be convenient, otherwise the business risks losing customers to competitors.
Customer engagement	This involves creating a positive experience for the customer when dealing with a business. This can include: • Attitude and behaviour of staff e.g. were they polite, knowledgeable, efficient, dressed appropriately? • Systems e.g. automated answer machines, online FAQs, contact details, payment procedures • Physical environment e.g. store layout, ease of use of an internet site, cleanliness of facilities, signage
Responses to customer feedback	Businesses get feedback from customers on a regular basis. It is important that they respond appropriately, without upsetting them. This requires a professional tone where the customer is treated with respect. The business should do its best to satisfy the customer. Dissatisfied customers are unlikely to be repeat buyers and the business will gain a poor reputation via word of mouth. This will lead to a reduction in revenue and a loss of potential new customers. With social media a bad reputation can spread quickly.
Post sales services	Many products require an ongoing service. A good website, online helpdesk and a reliable repair/support team can provide this. Post sales service includes: • User training • Help lines • Servicing

The benefits of good customer service include:
- Increase in customer satisfaction
  - Positive word of mouth advertising
  - No need to deal with complaints or angry customers
- Customer loyalty
  - Repeat business
  - Increased brand value
- Increased spend
  - Spend longer in store or online
  - Buy additional goods or services e.g. sales person explains benefit of an extended warranty
- Profitability
  - Increased revenue from repeat customers
  - More motivated workers who work harder and stay with the business longer

The dangers of poor customer service include:
- Dissatisfied customers
  - High number of complaints and returns
  - Demotivated staff dealing with unhappy customers, leading to increased absenteeism and high levels of labour turnover
- Poor reputation via word of mouth
  - Potential new customers unwilling to try the business
  - Increased need to spend on promotional activities in order to try and attract customers
- Reduction in revenue
  - Less repeat custom
  - Loss of potential new customers
  - High number of refunds or discounts offered to compensate for poor service

TalkTalk Group provides broadband services along with a range of other telecommunications. In 2018 it generated the highest volume of complaints per 100 000 subscribers for its broadband services. This was for the 2nd year running. Regulator Ofcom release this data in order to help consumers make better informed decisions. This is a competitive environment with a number of Broadband suppliers such as Sky, BT, Virgin and Plusnet. Therefore, it is important that these businesses address issues of poor customer service.

Test Yourself

2.3.4 The sales process

1. What is customer service?

2. What is the sales process?

3. State three methods of providing good customer service.

4. Explain why good product knowledge can improve the quality of customer service.

5. Explain why customer engagement can improve the quality of customer service.

6. Explain why good post sales service can improve the quality of customer service.

7. Explain how good service can increase customer loyalty.

8. Explain one financial benefit of good customer service.

9. Explain how poor customer service can damage the reputation of a business.

10. Explain one financial danger of poor customer service.

2.4.1 Business calculations

What you need to learn
- The concept and calculation of:
  - gross profit
  - net profit
- Calculation and interpretation of:
  - gross profit margin
  - net profit margin
  - average rate of return

An income statement
- Shows a summary of a firm's trading and expenses in a given time period (normally a year) in order to identify whether the business has made a profit or a loss

Components	What it shows
Revenue (sales)	The total amount of money achieved as a result of selling goods or services Calculated as quantity sold x selling price
Cost of sales (cost of goods sold)	The costs which are directly related to producing the goods or services sold e.g. raw materials
Gross profit	Revenue (**sales**) minus cost of sales (**cost of goods sold**)
Expenses	All indirect costs experienced by the business, not direct production costs
Net profit	Gross profit minus expenses

Example: Income statement of Jessica's Vegetarian Foods Ltd

		£	£
Revenue (**sales**)			250 000
less Cost of sales* (**cost of goods sold**)			130 000
Gross profit			120 000
Expenses*	Wages and salaries	45 000	
	Marketing	8 000	
	Rent and rates	12 000	
	Other expenses	2 500	67 500
Net profit			52 500

*Cost of sales and expenses may be presented as a total figure as shown here for cost of sales or listed as shown here for expenses

When interpreting an income statement businesses use two key measures of profitability. These are **gross profit margin** and **net profit margin**.

Gross profit margin	Net profit margin
Shows gross profit as a % of revenue (**sales**)	Shows net profit as a % of revenue (**sales**)
Formula*: $\dfrac{\text{Gross profit} \times 100}{\text{Revenue}}$	Formula*: $\dfrac{\text{Net profit} \times 100}{\text{Revenue}}$
Example: $\dfrac{120\,000 \times 100}{250\,000} = 48\%$	Example: $\dfrac{52\,500 \times 100}{250\,000} = 21\%$
For every £1 made in sales 48p is left as gross profit. A very low gross profit margin may indicate that the cost of sales is too high in relation to selling price.	For every £1 made in sales 21p is left as net profit. A very low net profit margin may indicate that the cost of sales and/or expenses are too high in relation to selling price.

*The formula will not be given to you in the exam

Investment projects are when a business spends funds on long term activities aimed to increase future revenue.

New machinery	New buildings	New vehicles
For example, a production line to increase the amount the business can produce or increase efficiency.	For example, to build a new factory to increase output or open new stores to reach more customers.	For example, a new fleet of delivery vans to improve distribution or launch a delivery service.

Investment projects often require large amounts of finance. The business must therefore be relatively confident that the investment is worthwhile.

In 2018 JCB announced an investment of over £50m in a new factory in Uttoxeter, Staffordshire, creating over 200 jobs by 2022. This will allow it to build driver cabs to go on its machines, such as diggers. The factory, opening in 2019, will increase capacity by 100 000 cabs a year. This will allow it to increase efficiency, improving quality whilst lowering unit costs.

Average rate of return (ARR) is an investment appraisal technique i.e. it is one way of assessing whether an investment is worthwhile. It allows for easy comparisons to be made between different investments. The higher the ARR figure the better. However, it gives no consideration to the timings of the inflow of cash e.g. early on in a project or towards the end of an investment. This can have a serious effect on cash flow.

ARR calculates average profit as a percentage of the initial cost of the investment.

The formula for ARR is:

> **Average annual profit/cost of investment × 100**

The formula for average annual profit is:

> **Total profit/number of years**

Worked example:

Worked example: A printing company is thinking of investing in a new machine at the cost of £25 000. It is estimated that this will increase profit by £6 000 per year for the first 2 years and £7 000 per year for the next 5 years. The machine has an expected life of 7 years.

Step 1: calculate the average annual profit:

Total profit / number of years

(£6 000 x 2) + (£7 000 x 5) / 7

= £47 000 / 7 = £6 714.28

Step 2: calculate ARR

Average annual profit / cost of investment × 100

£6 714.28/£25 000 x 100

= 26.8%

Making a profit is an important objective for businesses but sometimes, especially when a business is starting up. This might not be possible and so it will be satisfied in the short term with breaking even.

This means that the business is not making a profit or a loss. It is the point at which revenue is sufficient to cover all costs.

Test Yourself

2.4.1 Business calculations

1. What is the formula gross profit?

2. What is the formula for net profit?

3. What is its gross profit?

4. What is its net profit?

A business has sales revenue of £156 000, cost of sales of £89 000 and expenses of £42 000.

5. What is its gross profit margin?

6. What is its net profit margin?

7. State two examples of investment projects undertaken by a business.

8. What is the formula for average annual profit?

9. What is the formula for average rate of return?

10. An investment project costs £50 000. This will increase profits by £8 000 a year for 8 years. What is the ARR?

2.4.2 Understanding business performance

> **What you need to learn**
> - The use and interpretation of quantitative business data to support, inform and justify business decisions:
>   - information from graphs and charts
>   - financial data
>   - marketing data
>   - market data
> - The use and limitations of financial information in:
>   - understanding business performance
>   - making business decisions

The use and interpretation of quantitative business data

Research findings must be interpreted and used to inform decision making.

Results may be presented:
- Numerically
  - Statistics, tables, %
- Written form
  - Report, quotes
- Graphically
  - Pie chart, bar chart, line graph, map

Businesses use market research to help inform decision making. Their findings are presented in different formats. It is important to be able to interpret and use qualitative and quantitative research findings to help make appropriate decisions for different types of business. This requires the manipulation and interpretation of data from tables and charts.

Data is information i.e. facts and figures that have been collated in a way that allows them to be used to inform decision making. In business, research data is presented to key personnel. They will interpret this data to inform themselves of decisions that will impact the business in the future.

Data presented diagrammatically is easier to interpret and analyse than raw data. Two methods of presenting data are pie charts and bar charts.

Pie charts

A circle is divided into sections or slices, each section being proportional to the data that it represents. If the population was 60% male and 40% female the pie chart would show 60% of the circle as male and 40% as female. However, pie charts are not really useful when there are just two pieces of data; they provide a more meaningful visual when there are multiple pieces of data e.g. market research from different socio-economic groups as a proportion of all groups.

The following market research shows the market for crisps in the UK.

This information could be used to identify market share of the major brands in the UK. Here, we can see that Walkers dominates the market for crisps, with 58% market share.

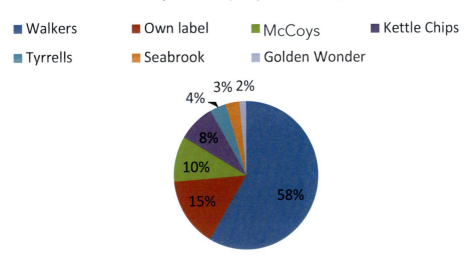

Edexcel GCSE (9-1) Business Theme 2

Bar charts

Bar charts are used when the outcomes show categories e.g. how many cars were red, blue or white. They show how frequently an outcome occurs when the data intervals are successive e.g. number of employees from 0 to 50.

Here, we can see the salaries of people who are customers of a business selling cars. 24 customers earn between £31 000 and £40 000.

How many customers earn more than £40 000? How might this market research be used to price products sold by the business?

Financial data

Keeps the business and other stakeholders informed about the business' financial performance:
- Identifies whether the business is making a profit or a loss
- Shows how much the business is worth

Financial data informs managers on the payment of suppliers and receipts from customers. It can help inform future decisions. It measures performance against alternative investment opportunities.

Marketing data
Keeps the business and other stakeholders informed about the business' marketing performance. Helps to identify:
- New product development
- Pricing strategies
- The mix of promotion methods to use
- Appropriate channels of distribution

Marketing data helps inform future decisions. It measures performance against alternative marketing opportunities.

Market data
Keeps the business and other stakeholders informed about the market.

Helps to identify:
- Market share
- Market size
- Market growth
- Information regarding current and potential competition

Informs managers on:
- The level of competition in the market
- New market development e.g. geographical or by product

Market data helps inform future decisions. It measures performance against alternative market opportunities.

Financial, marketing and market data allows stakeholders to assess current performance against:
- Past performance
- Targets
- Other businesses e.g. competitors

The use and limitations of financial information in:
Understanding business performance
A business has to record all transactions of money going into and out of the business. These transactions form a numerical history of the business and are summarised in its financial statements.

These inform the business and other stakeholders about the business' performance:
- Identifies whether the business is making a profit or a loss
- Shows how much the business is worth

Financial information tracks the flow of cash into and out of the business. It informs managers on the payment of suppliers and receipts from customers.

Making business decisions
One role of managers is decision making. Decisions can be scientific i.e. based on data or hunch i.e. based on intuition.

All decisions have an opportunity cost i.e. the cost of one decision in terms of the next best alternative foregone. All decisions carry risks and rewards as well as being based on uncertainty.

Scientific	Intuition
Supported by quantifiable evidence	Allows for quick decision making
Encourages a logical thought process	Encourages innovation and creativity
However:	However:
May require expensive data	Difficult to justify
Time consuming	Reliant on experience and expertise

If data is historic this is not always an accurate indication of the future. For example, costs may rise leading to future profit levels falling rather than continuing to grow or a new competitor may enter the market.

If data is for the future it is based on forecasts which may not be accurate. For example, ARR is based on predicted cash inflows and outflows over the life of the project.

It is important to remember that the data may have been manipulated. For example, a manager may present overly optimistic forecasts in order to convince directors to make an investment.

Test Yourself

2.4.2 Understanding business performance

1. What is data?

2. Explain one reason why pie charts are useful in displaying information.

3. Explain one reason why bar charts are useful in displaying information.

4. Explain one reason why the use of financial data is beneficial to a business.

5. Explain one reason why the use of marketing data is beneficial to a business.

6. Explain one reason why the use of market data is beneficial to a business.

7. Explain one use and one limitation of using financial information.

8. Distinguish between scientific and intuitive decision making.

9. Explain one problem of using historic data.

10. Explain one problem of using forecast data.

2.5.1 Organisational structures

What you need to learn
- Different organisational structures and when each are appropriate:
  - hierarchical and flat
  - centralised and decentralised
- The importance of effective communication:
  - the impact of insufficient or excessive communication on efficiency and motivation
  - barriers to effective communication
- Different ways of working:
  - part-time, full-time and flexible hours
  - permanent, temporary, and freelance contracts
  - the impact of technology on ways of working: efficiency, remote working

As a business grows it is likely to employ more people and therefore the organisation becomes more complex. It is more difficult to **communicate** with and **coordinate** all of the workers. A business will therefore develop a **structure** made up of **hierarchies** or levels.

Organisational structure is the way in which all of the people within the business, from directors and managers to all employees, are organised.
- It provides answers to the following questions:
  - Who does each worker report to?
  - Who is each manager responsible for?
  - How many levels are there?
  - How many departments are there?
  - How does communication flow?

Organisational trees are a visual representation of the organisational structure.

Layers of management are the number of levels in the organisational structure, these are also called hierarchies.
- The more layers the longer the communication flow
- Will affect the speed and accuracy with which information is passed through the organisation
- Can slow down decision making

Span of control is the number of people a manager is **directly** responsible for. In the diagram opposite, the top manager has a span of control of 4. There are 41 people in total below him or her in the structure, but they are only directly responsible for 4.
- The wider the span of control the more difficult it is for a manager to coordinate their team

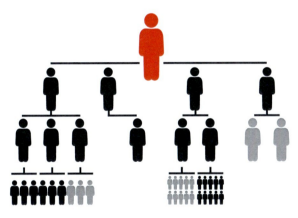

Chain of command is the route communication takes as it flows through a business.

Delayering involves removing a level of management from the hierarchy.

Delegation involves the passing of authority from a manager to a subordinate.

Businesses have internal organisational structures to help all employees understand their position in the hierarchy. This clarifies the flow of communication and authority. It helps understand different job roles.

Edexcel GCSE (9-1) Business Theme 2

Directors
Senior personnel at the top of the hierarchy.
Responsible for major decision and the overall vision of the business.
Managers
Responsible for decisions on a day to day basis.
Normally responsible for a specific function e.g. a marketing manager, a specific region e.g. London sales manager or product e.g. soft drinks manager.
Assistants reporting to a manager are normally responsible for their own work and not closely supervised.
Supervisors
Responsible for overviewing the work of a specific group of workers.
Often responsible for the close supervision of low or unskilled workers.
Subordinates
An employee who reports to someone higher up in the organisational structure.
Often have little responsibility for decision making.

The levels of hierarchy within businesses will differ.

Hierarchical organisational structures	Flat organisational structures
Each superior is responsible for a few subordinates. This allows for closer supervision and communication between the two levels.	Each superior is responsible for a large number of subordinates. This requires greater delegation but fewer levels, allowing for quicker communication throughout the business.
Narrow span of control.	Wide span of control.
Long chain of command.	Short chain of command.

The structure of the organisation will affect many aspects of how the workers are managed and treated, including:
- Degree of responsibility
- Level of supervision
- Training required
- Motivation
- Flow of communication
  - Speed and accuracy
- Opportunities for promotion
- Methods of communication

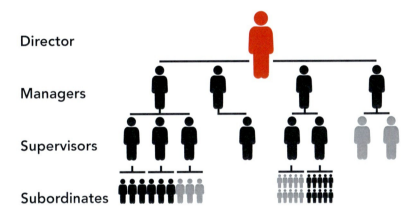

The organisational structure shows levels of management but this does not mean that managers at the top of the tree automatically make all the decisions. Responsibility for **decision making** can be shared between managers at lower levels. This depends upon whether decision making is **centralised** or **decentralised**.

The importance of effective communication

Organisational structure may affect the different ways of communication, including:

- Ease with which face to face communication can take place e.g. if a manager has a wide span of control it may be difficult to gather all subordinates together at one time
- Written communication to ensure important information does not get changed e.g. the Chinese whisper effect as communication travels down a long chain of command
- Use of ICT such as emails, Skype and video conferencing e.g. influenced by where employees are located
- Instant messaging (IM) is increasingly used in businesses as it is quick and can be used within a group of employees operating on the same project e.g. influenced by a specific job that is undertaken by a small group of workers, located in different areas
- The use of telephone and mobile phones to communicate e.g. when employees are travelling, such as on a train

In 2016 the Co-operative Group rebranded to become the Co-op. It wanted to reconnect with the 70 000 employees in its diverse organisation. These included those working in retailing, education, finance, insurance, legal and funeral care. The 'Back to being Co-op' campaign began with 90 minute face-to-face meetings at 130 locations, with employees integrated from a range of departments and levels of the hierarchy. By embracing social media all employees could be involved in the challenges faced by the business and could contribute their own ideas. #beingcoop was used to communicate employees' stories and to create a feeling of belonging within the business. 40 Co-op hosts travel the country every week, communicating the Co-op's rich history and support for communities.

To what extent has the organisational structure of the Co-op impacted on its communication methods?

Barriers to effective communication

There are a number of barriers stopping effective communication.

Physical barriers	Cultural barriers	Language barriers	Perception
Larger organisations operate in different locations, impacting on face to face discussions.	A clash of cultures might occur with different interpretations of messages. Or for businesses operating in different countries there may be a range of cultures affecting the way in which communication takes place and workforce practices.	Misunderstanding of words and instructions in a cosmopolitan workplace or when operating in a range of countries.	Employees may interpret the same message in different ways.

Different ways of working

The workforce may be on a full-time or part-time contract that stipulates the number of hours to be worked.
- Full-time is considered to be over 35 hours a week
- Part-time is considered to be less than 35 hours a week

Benefits of full-time employment	Benefits of part-time employment
Increased security for workers	Greater flexibility
Easier to feel part of a team	Wider pool of workers
Employees may be more committed	Helps keep valued workers within the business
Less people to supervise	Easier to respond to changes in demand
Lower recruitment and training costs	

Flexible hours

The employee can work hours that are different to the normal hours of the business. This might take the form of job sharing where hours and tasks are divided between employees. This might provide flexibility for employees and cost benefits for the business. The employee might work from home rather than the normal place of work. This has been made easier due to the internet.

Permanent contracts

Many employees are **permanent**. They have no specified termination date for their contract.

- These can either be part-time or full-time
- Permanent workers will spend more time in the job and will therefore have more scope to build up their knowledge base and working practices

Temporary contracts

Temporary employee is a person who is contracted to work for a business for a specified period of time e.g. 6 months to cover maternity leave.

- Temporary employees can be full-time or part-time and help meet the short term needs of a business
- They do not have the security that a permanent employee has
- Often, they are agency workers and are brought in to fill gaps at peak times e.g. seasonal work or to cover peak holiday periods

Freelance contracts

Freelance workers tend to be self-employed. They are likely to run their own business and have a number of different clients at the same time.
- They decide when and where they want to work
- Reputation is important if they are to get repeat custom
- They are often specialists and can be called in to the business to help with issues where there is not the appropriate expertise. Therefore, they may be expensive

A business is likely to use a mixture of workers in order to operate on a day to day basis.

The impact of technology on ways of working: efficiency and remote working

Developments in ICT have aided business communications, reducing the need for business travel and allowing people to change the way they work. This has included:
- Mobile phones
- Web conferencing / online meetings / desktop sharing
- Broadband / telephone advances e.g. Skype
- Social media
- Cloud storage e.g. Dropbox
- E Mail

However there are issues:
- Cost of installing and staying current
- Need to train staff
- Loss of personal contact
- Data overload

Test Yourself

2.5.1 Organisational structures

1. What are organisational structures?

2. What is a span of control?

3. What is a chain of command?

4. With reference to organisational structure explain the different job roles that exist in a business.

5. Distinguish between a flat and a tall organisational structure.

6. Explain how organisational structure can affect the different ways of communicating.

7. Explain one advantage and one disadvantage of centralisation.

8. Explain one advantage and one disadvantage of decentralisation.

9. Explain one benefit of the following types of working contract:
    a. Part-time
    b. Full-time
    c. Flexible hours
    d. Permanent
    e. Temporary
    f. Freelance

10. Explain one impact of technology on ways of working.

2.5.2 Effective recruitment

> **What you need to learn**
> - Different job roles and responsibilities:
>   - key job roles and their responsibilities: directors, senior managers, supervisors/team leaders, operational and support staff
> - How businesses recruit people:
>   - documents: person specification and job description, application form, CV
>   - recruitment methods used to meet different business needs (internal and external recruitment)

Recruitment is the process of identifying a vacancy in the workforce and the steps taken to attract the right quality of worker to fill this vacancy.

Why do firms need to recruit?
A business will recruit new workers for a variety of reasons:
- The business is growing
- To replace an employee who has left
- New skills required
- Increased workload
- Covering positions on a temporary basis

Recruitment can be:
- **Internal** – appointing an existing employee to a new role
- **External** – appointing an employee from outside of the business

Employing the correct people is important to the success of a business. Businesses therefore follow a process when recruiting new employees.

Businesses employ a variety of workers. These include:

Directors

These are a part of the top level decision-making team and sit on the board of directors. They are responsible for medium to long term decisions within the business. This decision-making will have a significant impact on the long term success of the business. Directors tend to be in charge of a specific functional area e.g. finance or marketing.

Senior managers

These are in charge of a number of subordinates and have responsibility for short to medium term decision making. Management is the process through which company resources are used and decisions made in order to meet the objectives of the business. Managers will set objectives and decide how to go about achieving them.

The role of senior management includes:

- Planning
- Organising
- Monitoring and evaluating
- Reporting

Supervisors

These are in charge of a group of employees undertaking specific tasks. They are likely to lead a department within an organisation and lead a number of subordinates within that department. The role entails closely monitoring the work of subordinates. This is a lower level management position often responsible for low skilled workers.

Operational and support staff

Operational staff are the core workers of a business. They carry out the main activities e.g. teachers in a school or machine operators in a factory. Support staff carry out work that is necessary for the business to function but are not directly related to the operations of the business. They might help operational staff in their day to day business e.g. a teaching assistant. The tasks that they undertake are secondary to the main operations of the business. They might do necessary jobs that are important to the smooth running of the business e.g. ancillary workers in hospitals who might change bed sheets, clean wards or cook food.

The main stages in the recruitment and selection process	
Job analysis	Once a vacancy has been identified a business will look to find out exactly what it requires e.g. number of hours, skills and place in the organisational structure. This will then lead to identifying a suitable pay level.
Job description	A document outlining the roles and responsibilities that the successful candidate will have to perform. This will include job title, place in the organisational structure and specific duties to be carried out.
Person specification	A document outlining what type of person is required. This will include skills, qualifications, characteristics and personality. This may be divided into essential and desirable.
Selection methods	Techniques used to identify the best person for the position. Selection methods include: • Application forms, curriculum vitae and covering letters • Interviews which can be face to face, telephone or online e.g. Skype • Tests e.g. workplace activities or psychometric tests

Application form	Curriculum Vitae (CV)
• Produced by the business • Completed by the candidate • Combination of open and closed questions • Submitted on paper or online	• Produced by the candidate • Standard recommended formats but each one will be different • May be accompanied with a covering letter of application

An effective recruitment and selection process will help ensure a business has the right number of workers with the right skills to fulfil their jobs efficiently and hence help a business achieve its objectives.

Factors contributing to this will include:
- Right skills and attitude
- Motivated
- Care about their job and the business
- Fit into the team

The benefits of having an effective recruitment and selection process include:

- **High productivity** resulting from having employees with the right skills to be able to carry out their jobs effectively
- **High quality output** as employees are committed to producing high quality goods with reduced waste
- **Customer service** will be improved as staff will be well informed and happy in the workplace
- **Staff retention** will increase with employees suited to the job and wanting to stay with the business for longer

Once a suitable candidate has been recruited the employer will issue the employee with a contract of employment. This is a formal document that sets out an agreement between the employer and the employee. For example, hours of work, responsibilities, rights and wages.

Drawbacks of internal recruitment	Drawbacks of external recruitment
Limited pool of applicants	Expensive recruitment costs
Employees who do not gain a promotion may be demotivated	Employee is not known to the business
Lack of new ideas coming into the business	May alienate internal candidates
May find it difficult to supervise previous colleagues	May take time to understand how the business works

Test Yourself

2.5.2 Effective recruitment

1. What is the role of a director?

2. Distinguish between a manager and supervisor.

3. What are operational workers?

4. What is meant by recruitment?

5. Distinguish between an application form and a CV.

6. Identify two benefits to a business of effective recruitment.

7. What is internal recruitment?

8. What is external recruitment?

9. Explain one benefit and one drawback of internal recruitment.

10. Explain one benefit and one drawback of external recruitment.

2.5.3 Effective training and development

> **What you need to learn**
> - How businesses train and develop employees:
>   - different ways of training and developing employees: formal and informal training, self-learning, ongoing training for all employees, use of target setting and performance reviews
> - Why businesses train and develop employees:
>   - the link between training, motivation and retention
>   - retraining to use new technology

Training is the range of activities undertaken to equip employees with the skills necessary to carry out their jobs effectively.

Training can be for new employees to learn the necessary skills or for existing employees to improve their skills or learn new ones.

The British Airways (BA) Global Learning Academy trains employees in a range of fields such as piloting and cabin crew. The latter provide the first impression for the airline. Invariably, they are perfectly turned out, have impeccable manners and provide for a calm experience. This is particularly important when customers might be scared to fly, in a rush or feeling unwell after a stressful business trip or holiday. Behind the cool but friendly demeanour of the hostess is hours of training to cover a range of emergencies. Similarly, potential pilots undergo hours of training on BA's 15 flight simulators, whilst existing pilots update their skills twice a year. With over 40 000 employees, in an industry where health and safety are essential, training and retraining are seen as a priority.

Different ways of training and developing employees

Formal training involves being taught systematically by a teacher. Training is split into segments and there is progression within a course. It is mainly delivered to groups and allows employees to learn about specific areas associated with the job. Understanding can be updated on a regular basis to take account of new information. Often, specialists will deliver the training within the business.

However, employees might be sent on courses e.g. day courses or day release, perhaps at a university, over a longer period of time.

Informal training does not follow a systematic structure. It involves training as and when it is required e.g. a new computer system in the workplace. It can be delivered through work colleagues or by specialists brought in to discuss a specific subject. It can also be more personal, with employees receiving the training from colleagues that they trust and respect. Examples include discussions with, or observations of, workmates to see how they approach specific tasks.

Self-learning involves ongoing education without the support of a teacher or educational institution. Many employees will have developed the ability to self-educate by the time they have entered the workplace. As the individual becomes more independent, they can access information from a wide variety of formats such as newspapers and specialist magazines. In particular, the Internet has provided an enormous amount of information for employees to undertake wider reading or learn through watching videos.

On-going training for all employees as training should not be seen as a one off at the start of a new job. It should be ongoing to continue to develop employees and keep them motivated. Re-training may be necessary as the work place changes:
- New legislation e.g. health and safety
- New technology
- New products or processes
- New government training schemes

Life-long learning aims to promote active learning and career development for all regardless of age.

Use of target setting and performance reviews involves reviewing the performance of staff against pre-agreed targets. Staff appraisals take place to look at the performance of staff over a period of time. Management will review performance against the targets that were agreed during a previous appraisal. Pay may be partly based on performance (Performance Related Pay) as measured by the staff appraisal. This can help to identify potential candidates for promotion and allows the business to identify problem areas with staff. The business can then take action to reduce these problems, maybe by arranging for additional training or support. These performance reviews give both parties an opportunity to discuss training needs.

Why businesses train and develop employees

The link between training, motivation and retention

Increased motivation as the workforce feels cared for and respected, this leads to higher productivity and lower turnover. Employees have better skills and are therefore better able to carry out their tasks which leads to greater output and less mistakes. Therefore, they have greater satisfaction in their job role.

Staff retention as workers feel that they have a future in the business, with opportunities to improve their skills and progress within the organisational structure. Informed workers who offer good product knowledge and are trained to help customers are likely to stay within the business.

Retraining to use new technology

Employees need retraining to be able to deal with constant changes in technology. As technology develops or new equipment is introduced to the workplace employees will need to learn how to use these. Businesses must ensure that employees are kept up to date with these changes to ensure the production of high-quality goods. There will be improved quality of output due to better skills and less mistakes. This can give a business a competitive advantage as customers are more likely to pay higher prices for products that have been created with, or incorporate, the latest technology.

Test Yourself

2.5.3 Effective training and development

1. What is training?

2. Explain one reason why training staff can give a business a competitive advantage.

3. Distinguish between formal and informal training.

4. What is self-learning?

5. Explain one reason why on-going training for all employees is necessary in a business.

6. Explain one reason why target setting might benefit a business.

7. State two benefits for a business of carrying out performance reviews.

8. Explain one reason why training can lead to motivation of the workforce.

9. Explain one reason why training can lead to retention of the workforce.

10. Explain why staff need retraining due to changes in technology.

2.5.4 Motivation

> **What you need to learn**
> - The importance of motivation in the workplace:
>   - attracting employees, retaining employees, productivity
> - How businesses motivate employees:
>   - financial methods: remuneration, bonus, commission, promotion, fringe benefits
>   - non-financial methods: job rotation, job enrichment, autonomy

Motivation can be defined as the reasons why a person does something.

Businesses will try to motivate workers to meet targets that will benefit the firm. Motivated staff are vital to the success of a business.

The importance of motivation in the workplace

Attracting employees will be easier as the business gains a good reputation. This will lead to a greater pool of workers, both skilled and unskilled, that would offer themselves for work.

Retaining employees as the workforce enjoy their job and are more likely to stay in the business, reducing recruitment costs and creating a more effective workforce.

Productivity will increase as motivated employees are likely to work harder. This means that their output will be higher. Therefore, output per worker will increase in the business as a whole. This is important as higher productivity will lead to a fall in unit costs. Thus, the business will have a competitive advantage. Alongside this, employees are likely to produce better quality products as they take more of a pride in the work that they undertake.

How businesses motivate employees

Financial incentives are the variety of methods that have a money value and are used to reward the workforce and influence their behaviour at work.

Financial methods include:

Remuneration is the main financial motivation for working. It can take a variety of forms:
- Wages where workers are paid a set hourly rate
- Salaries where workers are paid a set amount per month
- Piece rate where workers are paid per unit of output. This leads to employees working as hard as they can to increase their income. However, it can lead to issues over quality

A **bonus** is an additional, lump sum, one off payment to an employee for meeting individual, team or company targets. This:
- Makes employees work harder
- Costs the business only if targets are met
- Can demotivate staff if targets are not met

Commission is when payment is based on the number of units sold. This:
- May make employees work harder to achieve sales
- May lead to lower quality and reputation as employees seek to make sales at any cost

Promotion occurs when an employee gets a job role that is higher up the hierarchy of the business.
- This will include an increase in both pay and responsibility
- This provides a sense of achievement for the employee
- It is likely that employees will work hard to gain promotion, benefitting the business
- However, it can create rivalry and friction in the workplace, particularly when employees believe themselves to be better equipped for the job than the person who actually got the promotion

Fringe benefits are payments in kind. This means that they do not take the form of money, but they do have a money value. There are a number of fringe benefits, but the main ones include company cars, private health care e.g. BUPA, gym membership and pension schemes.

Non-financial incentives are the methods of motivating employees through elements of job design.

Non-financial methods include:

Job rotation involves varying the tasks that an employee does to reduce boredom and increase the range of skills that they have i.e. multi-tasking. Tasks undertaken will have the same level of responsibility, leading to greater job satisfaction as the employee has a change of job and, perhaps, scenery. It exposes the employee to a variety of jobs which might lead to them specialising in an area that they enjoy, or are good at, in the future.

Job enrichment involves an increase in the level of responsibility that an employee has. This increases job satisfaction as the employee takes more important decisions. It is likely to be accompanied by an increase in pay and lead to greater self-esteem and ability to achieve work related goals.

Autonomy is the degree to which the employee has independence, and can make decisions, in the workplace. This gives the employee greater freedom to be their own boss. Therefore, they can make decisions as they see fit. This means that the employee is more likely to be skilled and experienced. There will be less close supervision and a feeling of being valued and respected by the business.

Test Yourself

2.5.4 Motivation

1. What is motivation?

2. Explain one reason why motivation will help attract and retain employees.

3. Explain one reason why motivation will increase productivity.

4. What is remuneration?

5. Distinguish between a wage and a salary.

6. Explain how the following forms of financial methods motivate employees:
    a. Bonus
    b. Commission
    c. Promotion

7. Explain the benefits of motivated employees.

8. Explain one benefit of job rotation to a business.

9. Explain one benefit of job enrichment to an employee.

10. What is autonomy?